MENSA
Word
Puzzles
for Kids

THIS IS A CARLTON BOOK

Text and puzzle content copyright
© British Mensa Limited 1994 &
1997
Design and artwork copyright ©
Carlton Books Limited 1994 & 1997

This edition published by Carlton
Books Limited 1997

A CIP catalogue for this book is
available from the British Library

ISBN 1-85868-314-9

Printed and bound in Great Britain

MENSA
Word
Puzzles
for Kids

Robert Allen

CARLTON

INTRODUCTION

I suppose you're not going to read this, are you? I mean, I don't blame you or anything, I'd probably do the same in your place. If you like messing about with words then by now you'll have plunged into the book and be unscrambling anagrams, crossing crosswords, sorting syllables and generally having fun. The puzzles are divided into six levels of difficulty from easy, Level A, to almost impossible, Level F. Work your way through each level. Even if the higher levels seem really difficult now, once you've done a few easier ones they'll seem less daunting.

Of course, if you don't like words and a well-meaning relative bought this for you because they thought it was educational, then I'm sorry. It's not supposed to be educational. I hope it's engrossing, enchanting, delightful, tantalizing, tormenting and mind-bending. Have a quick look at the puzzles anyway. You never know, you might find out that you do like words after all.

Many thanks to my friend Sarah Picken for all her help in compiling this book.

R. P. Allen

Robert Allen
Editorial Director
Mensa Publication

How To Join MENSA

If you like puzzles then you would probably like Mensa.
It is the only society I know of which lets you in just
because you are good at puzzling. We have about 120,000
members throughout the world (with the majority in
Great Britain and the USA.). Junior members of British
Mensa keep in touch through *Bright Sparks* magazine
which appears bi-monthly and contains stories, puzzles,
features, a Rage Page (for the seriously enraged), letters,
perplexing questions with (we hope) sensible answers,
and lots more. The great thing about Mensa is that you
get to meet so many people with different interests. For
any more information contact British Mensa Limited,
Mensa House, St John's Square, Wolverhampton WV2
4AH.

THUMB SUCKERS

★ LEVEL A ★

PUZZLE 1

Below you'll find a pyramid. Using the clues,
fill in the correct words. To help you, to make the
new word a letter is added to the end of the
previous word each time.

1. A term of endearment for your father.

2. You can cook dinner in this.

3 Found in a window.

4. A group of entertainers appearing as contestants in a TV quiz show.

ANSWER NO.54

PUZZLE 2

The sentence below is a well known quotation.
We have used a simple trick to obscure the meaning.
Can you unscramble it?

WTOB ABEL FORC GNOTH ATOS OBER, ATHATI HIST ATHEM BQUESTIONA.

ANSWER NO.63

PUZZLE 3

If you fill the four words into the grid in the correct order, something found on the beach will be revealed in the shaded column. What is it?

S	H	O	P
A	W	a	y
N	E	E	D
D	O	w	n

NEED   **AWAY**

DOWN   **SHOP**

ANSWER NO.81

PUZZLE 4

When animals are grouped together we have some very interesting names to describe the groups, for example a murder of crows. Here are some easy ones to get you started.

A – – – – of cows.

A – – – – – – of hens.

A – – – – – – of geese.

A – – – – – of lions.

A – – – – – – of fish.

ANSWER NO. 116

PUZZLE 5

Below you will find a number of characters from books and rhymes whose names have been mixed up. Can you put them together again and find the odd one out?

CAPTAIN

CHRISTOPHER

PETER

MOTHER

PAN

BETTY

ROBIN

HUMPTY

GOOSE

HOOK

BOTTER

LUCY

DUMPTY

ANSWER NO.18

PUZZLE 6

The faces below have been made up out of letters. If you unravel them you will find the names of the people.

ANSWER NO.99

PUZZLE 7

What kind of a father goes round dressed all in red,
and never cuts his beard, and works only one day a
year? Unjumble the letters and you will find out.

FATHER HSARSMITC

? ANSWER NO.36 **?**

PUZZLE 8

Below you'll find anagrams of four common pets.
Which ones?

LEVEL A

1. tca

2. dgo

3. hifs

4. sahmter

? ANSWER NO.167 **?**

PUZZLE 9

One of these tins of paint does not
go with the others, which is it?

PURPLE

INDIGO

RED

GREEN

PIMENTO

◆?◆ ANSWER NO. 125 ◆?◆

PUZZLE 10

The clues below will help you to find words to fill the spaces. To help you even more we can tell you that the first syllable of each word could be found in a paint box.

Villain	B					U		

Fruit	B		U				R	

Plan					P			T

Famous pirate		L				B		R	

For growing plants			E			H			E

ANSWER NO.142

LEVEL A

PUZZLE 11

Who ate the grapes? Look at the word and see if you can find a four-letter word describing the culprits.

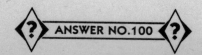 ANSWER NO.27

PUZZLE 12

Have you had enough of school? Well, just unravel the jumbled letters and add them to the word play.
Then relax.

PLAY EMIT

ANSWER NO.100

PUZZLE 13

The bear had a sore head. He was not in a good mood. In fact he was in a really awful mood. Take the jumbled letters below and add them to the word bear to make one word which will show you just how bad he was feeling.

E B N

L A U

- - BEAR - - - -

ANSWER NO.45

PUZZLE 14

Fill in the words in the correct order and in the shaded column you will be able to see something that comes out at night.

FORK   KNEE

POLE

ANSWER NO.80

If you solve these anagrams you will reveal four
numbers. What is the total of all the numbers
added together?

1. ofur

2. vesen

3. noe

4. ixs

LEVEL A

PUZZLE 16

Look at the words on the chalk board, which is the odd one out?

ANSWER NO.9

PUZZLE 17

When rearranged, the anagrams below will turn into four types of weather. Can you work out what they are?

1. **arin**

2. **usn**

3. **nsow**

4. **ahil**

LEVEL A

? ANSWER NO.124 ?

PUZZLE 18

Mrs Jones was very proud of her garden. She had the best asters in the county. That is until next door's dog decided to bury his bone under them. Add the three jumbled up letters to the front of the word aster and make a new word telling you what happened.

- - - ASTER

PUZZLE 19

The faces below have been made up out of letters. If you unravel them you will find the names of the people.

LEVEL A

ANSWER NO. 168

The birds were just enjoying a few well-earned crumbs in the garden when along came that mean and murderous cat from the house round the corner. What did the birds do? Add the jumbled letters to the word cat and you will get the answer.

R S

E T

– C A T – – –

◆ ANSWER NO. 64 ◆

PUZZLE 21

If you fill in these four words correctly you will find a type of flower in the shaded column.

BOOK **CHEF**

VASE **BIRD**

ANSWER NO. 151

PUZZLE 22

At the zoo the monkeys were throwing oranges at each other. If you look closely at the word orange you will see a three-letter word which tells you what the keeper did.

ANSWER NO.53

PUZZLE 23

The planets in the night sky have an intruder among them. Which is it?

EARTH

MARS

VERMICELLI

SATURN

MERCURY

 ANSWER NO.62

PUZZLE 24

Can you find the word ELEMENT? It appears only once in a horizontal, vertical or diagonal line.

E	L	M	E	N	T	E	L	E	M
L	E	E	L	E	N	M	E	N	T
M	E	N	T	E	L	M	E	N	T
E	L	E	M	E	N	E	L	M	E
E	M	E	N	T	E	L	E	M	E
L	M	E	L	E	M	E	M	T	N
E	E	L	M	E	N	T	E	L	E
M	N	T	E	L	E	M	N	E	T
E	T	E	M	E	N	E	T	L	E
N	E	L	E	M	E	N	E	N	T

THUMB SUCKERS

◇ ? ANSWER NO. 82 ? ◇

PUZZLE 25

It's bedtime but are you sleepy? No! Now what should
we try? Unravel the letters below and you will come
up with a suggestion.

BEDTIME

ROTSY

LEVEL A

◆?◆ ANSWER NO.115 ◆?◆

PUZZLE 26

Can you solve these anagrams to reveal four
well-known parts of the body?

1. ram

2. ahed

3. elg

4. ofot

ANSWER NO. 17

PUZZLE 27

This is one strange dog! If you take the two groups of mixed-up letters and add one to the front and one to the end you will come up with the seven-letter names of two very different creatures.

L L
U B

– D O G –

I F
H S

ANSWER NO. 35

PUZZLE 28

Place the words into the grid in such a way that
something hot can be seen in the shaded column.

ACHE   WOLF

HAIR   TAXI

ANSWER NO. 126

PUZZLE 29

Look carefully at the caterpillar. See if you can find a three-letter word which tells you what happened to the apple. Caterpillars should only eat leaves, so he felt sick. See if you can also find a four-letter word which tells what he took to feel better.

CATERPILLAR

PUZZLE 30

Take a look at the names on the children's school bags. Which is the odd one out?

THUMB SUCKERS

ANSWER NO. 26

PUZZLE 31

Milo got into old Mr Jimson's orchard and guzzled his peaches happily all afternoon. But that night the fruit had its revenge! Take a look at the word peaches and try to find a five-letter word which describes just how Milo's tummy felt.

ANSWER NO.79

LEVEL A

PUZZLE 32

Now we're really going to rock you! But how? With a track from the latest album by Total Cosmic Disaster? Aren't you just a little young for that kind of music? Why not just rearrange the jumbled letters below and come up with a swinging solution.

ROCKING SRHOE

ANSWER NO.97

PUZZLE 33

Teddy isn't a boy and he isn't a dog, he isn't a
tomato and he isn't a frog. If you unravel the letters
with care you will discover that he is a...

TEDDY AREB

ANSWER NO.166

PUZZLE 34

It was the highlight of the display. A giant
firework! But what sort was it going to be?
Just unscramble the letters below to find
the answer.

CATHERINE
LEWEH

ANSWER NO.44

PENCIL CHEWERS

★ LEVEL B ★

PUZZLE 35

Look at the farm gate. It may look like alphabet soup to you but, if you start with the first H and then take every fifth letter, you will be able to find an animal who lives on the farm. Try again starting with the G, then the M and so on. There are five hidden animals.

ANSWER NO.8

PUZZLE 36

Walter Foole has taken a job at the local library. Oh
well, once a Foole always a Foole and he has already
accidentally removed the name labels from several
shelves. Try to sort them all out before the librarian
finds out and marks Walter's card.

PENCIL CHEWERS

THE HOBBIT	JAMES AND THE GIANT PEACH
MARK TWAIN	TOVE JANNSON

FINN FAMILY MOOMINTROLL	TOM SAWYER
JACK LONDON	A.A. MILNE

THE HOUSE AT POOH COR-NER	WHITE FANG
ROALD DAHL	J.R.R. TOLKIEN

◆?◆ ANSWER NO.123 ◆?◆

PUZZLE 37

Replace each question mark with a letter to form a word. Reading down you should discover the names of five things to be found in a kitchen. What are they?

WA	?	ER
DI	?	TY
RA	?	NY
WE	?	GE
AN	?	ER
KN	?	AD

JU	?	BO
GR	?	ND
PA	?	ED
AR	?	AY
AB	?	VE
MO	?	ED
CR	?	CK
RI	?	ET
FR	?	AK

HI	?	ER
AM	?	ND
OU	?	ER
EX	?	RA
SA	?	TY
ST	?	RN

HU	?	KY
CR	?	NE
AC	?	TE
IN	?	UR
TH	?	ME
VE	?	GE

BL	?	OD
MO	?	IE
FR	?	SH
MA	?	IA

ANSWER NO.140

PUZZLE 38

All the well-known sayings have a word missing.
Complete them by taking words from the group on
the right.

1. Too many chiefs and not enough ?

2. Many hands make ? work

3. An ? a day keeps the doctor away

4. A new broom ? clean

5. A stitch in time saves ?

6. Cut your coat according to your ?

7. When the ? away the mice will play

8. Can't see the wood for the ?

9. All's well that ends?

10. It's an ill ? that blows nobody any good

ANSWER NO.169

PUZZLE 39

The letters on the computer screen make a series.
Work out the logic and replace the question mark.

MTW
TFS?

ANSWER NO.65

PUZZLE 40

The answers to the six clues below are all anagrams
of each other. What are they?

Small piece of wire driven
through sheets of paper to
hold them together ....

A crayon for drawing ....

The lightest hue ....

You eat off them ....

Folds often found in a
girl's skirt ....

The leaves of a flower ....

⟨?⟩ ANSWER NO. 152 ⟨?⟩

PUZZLE 41

Each of the following sets of clues should give you a pair of homophones (words that sound the same but have different meanings).

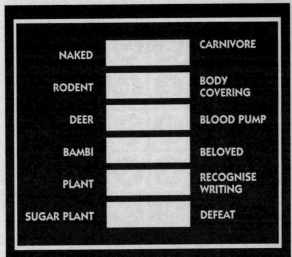

NAKED		CARNIVORE
RODENT		BODY COVERING
DEER		BLOOD PUMP
BAMBI		BELOVED
PLANT		RECOGNISE WRITING
SUGAR PLANT		DEFEAT

LEVEL B

? ANSWER NO.52 ?

PUZZLE 42

The diagram shows a plan of the secret headquarters of the dreaded Crime Syndicate International. By following the instructions clearly you can reach the Boss's office and apprehend him. Exciting, isn't it?

A	B	C
D	E	F
G	H	I
J	K	L
M	N	O
P	Q	R

N
W ↑ E
S

PENCIL CHEWERS

Start at the square two places south of the one in the middle of the top line. Go 1 square east and 2 south. Now go 2 squares west and 4 north. The room you want is now 1 square SE.

Which is the final square?

ANSWER NO.61

PUZZLE 43

The following sentence has two gaps which can be
filled with words using the same seven letters.

The _ _ _ _ _ _ _

felt lonely on the

frontier and longed

for _ _ _ _ _ _ _

from home.

LEVEL B

ANSWER NO.83

PUZZLE 44

Add a letter anywhere along the length of each word to make another word which fits the clue. Taking the added letters in order, the name of a girl will be revealed. Which one?

☐ 1. SELL — an odour

☐ 2. MAD — a female servant

☐ 3. HEAP — not expensive

☐ 4. TANK — to show your gratitude

☐ 5. PACE — opposite of war

☐ 6. FOG — to beat severely

☐ 7. WED — to fuse bits of metal together by heating

☐ 8. BARD — hair found on the face

B

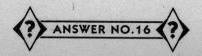

ANSWER NO.16

PUZZLE 45

Replace each question mark with a letter to form a word. Reading down you should discover the names of five jobs. What are they?

ER	?	SE
MI	?	RO
FA	?	ET
CH	?	RE
RO	?	TE
FI	?	AL
WA	?	CH
GR	?	DE
PI	?	CH
WI	?	CH

AM	?	LE
FR	?	SK
HO	?	LY
SH	?	RN
WI	?	TY

PI	?	CH
ER	?	PT
FA	?	CE
AI	?	LE
CH	?	AP

VI	?	AL
GR	?	ET
DR	?	WN
UL	?	ER
ET	?	IC
GL	?	AM
HO	?	SE

JU	?	GE
WH	?	RL
PA	?	TE
NI	?	HE
MA	?	OR
BR	?	WN
DE	?	AY
JO	?	ER
EV	?	NT
RO	?	AL

LEVEL B

ANSWER NO.114

PUZZLE 46

The creepie crawlies pictured have their names listed in code. Just to make the game more interesting we have mixed them all up. Leaving out "J", create a 5 x 5 grid with the letters A–E being A1 to A5, F–K B1 to B5, etc. Use these codes to solve the puzzle.

B

1. A5.A1.D2.E2.B4.B2

2. A3.A5.C3.D4.B4.C5.A5.A4.A5

3. D4.A1.D2.A1.C3.D4.D5.C1.A1

4. A3.C4.A3.B5.D2.C4.A1.A3.B3

5. A5.A1.D2.D4.B3.E2.C4.D2.C2

ANSWER NO.101

Can you work out the five words below?

LEVEL B

	a	b	c	d	e
1	T	R	I	Y	D
2	O	L	A	G	P
3	W	E	H	N	S

1. 3D 3B 1C 2D 3C

2. 3E 3D 2A 3A 1D

3. 1B 3B 2C 1E 1D

4. 1A 3C 2A 1B 3D

5. 2B 2C 1B 2D 3B

ANSWER NO.34

PUZZLE 48

We have taken some common expressions and mixed them up. Try to sort them into their proper sequence.

TO
SWIM
CATS
AND
DOGS

TO
SMELL
LIKE
A
BIRD

TO
FLY
LIKE
A
ROSE

TO
RUN
LIKE
A
FISH

TO
RAIN
LIKE
THE
WIND

ANSWER NO. 127

PUZZLE 49

The following are nicknames which have been mixed up. Some of them belong to things and some to people. When you have sorted them out you should find one pair which doesn't fit.

BIG   BRIAN

OLD   BEARD

UNION   NORMAN

BLUE   GLORY

GREEN   BEN

STORMIN'   JACK

? ANSWER NO.144 ?

PUZZLE 50

Find the letter to place at the centre of the wheel
which will turn all the spokes into five-letter words.
Each word starts with the same letter.

ANSWER NO. 165

PUZZLE 51

In a twisted, mind-bending sort of way the following words form a series. Which is the odd one out?

Adverb

Card

Engulf

Become

Grouch

LEVEL B

? ANSWER NO.25 ?

PUZZLE 52

In Madame Twoswords' famous waxworks Walter Foole, the newest assistant, has mixed up the labels on the dummies. Can you sort them out and help this dummy keep his job?

OLIVER	WASHINGTON
MAHATMA	ROBERTS
MICHELLE	CROMWELL
GEORGE	GANDHI
ROBIN	PFEIFFER
JULIA	CODY
WILLIAM	HOOD

ANSWER NO.43

Add one letter to each line which will end the left word and start the right word, changing both into new English words. Reading down, a popular star from the world of sport will be revealed. Which one?

SAG	?	WASH
THROW	?	ARROW
FIRE	?	ARK
PRIME	?	ANGER
HER	?	LOPE
DRAM	?	VERSION
BE	?	RATE
ARE	?	BATE
FORGE	?	CUBA
PEN	?	LEDGE
YET	?	RATE

LEVEL B

ANSWER NO. 78

PUZZLE 54

The answers to the five clues below are all anagrams of one another. What are the words?

Something left over . . . .

Fruits that grow
on trees . . . .

He clears the field
of a crop. . . . .

She cuts off the
outer surface. . . . .

Ancient battle
weapon . . . .

ANSWER NO.96

PUZZLE 55

The answers to the five clues below all rhyme.
What are they?

1. Unswerving
   in allegiance.

2. To ruin.

3. Their blood
   might be blue.

4. Hard work.

5. Grotesque
   spout on roof.

ANSWER NO.139

LEVEL B

B

PUZZLE 56

It is now Walter's second day working at the
world renowned waxworks of Madame Twoswords
and he's gone and mixed up the first names and
surnames of the models. Having sorted the labels into
equal piles, can you help put them in the right order
before Madame has poor Walter coated in wax and
put on display.

JOHN	ARMSTRONG
BONHAM-CARTER	EINSTEIN
ALBERT	NEIL
TAYLOR	BONAPARTE
HELENA	RICHARD
LENNON	GERE
ELIZABETH	NAPOLEON

PENCIL CHEWERS

? ANSWER NO.7 ?

PUZZLE 57

The answers to these ten clues all rhyme.
What are they?

1. Reptile or unpleasant person.

2. A dull persistent pain.

3. One way to cook potatoes.

4. An implement used in the garden.

5. To rouse from sleep

6. To abandon someone.

7. A large body of water.

8. To fracture an arm.

9. Marker in the ground.

10. To falsify.

LEVEL B

? ANSWER NO.122 ?

PUZZLE 58

You are hunting the autograph of Mucho Macho the film star. You know the right street but not the number. Here are some clues to help you find the house.

1. Mucho is much too macho to have flowers in his garden.

2. The number of the house cannot be divided by 7.

3. The house is not called Sunshine Cottage.

4. If the house number is divided by two the result is between 15 and 17.

5. Mucho made a film called 'Moon Mission'. It bombed.

6. Mucho is a known cat lover.

ANSWER NO. 170

NAIL NIBBLERS

★ LEVEL C ★

PUZZLE 59

The following strings of letters are all anagrams of well known cities. But each one contains an extra letter. Throw all the extra letters in the bin and you will have the name of one of the States of America.

dilnono

rapids

amore

shallad

oookyt

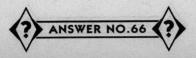
ANSWER NO.66

PUZZLE 60

Remove ten letters to leave a dead language.

PUZZLE 61

The following groups of letters are all names of countries from which two-letter 'heads' and 'tails' have been removed. How many can you recognise?

– – RTUG – –

– – NGA – –

– – MAN – –

– – RMA – –

– – EE – –

ANSWER NO.60

PUZZLE 62

Solve the clues and write the answers in the appropriate boxes. The right-hand answer will always be the same as the left-hand answer, except that one letter will be missing. Write the missing letter in the box on the far right, and reading down you will discover the name of a sauce.

1		2		
3		4		
5		6		
7		8		
9		10		
11		12		
13		14		
15		16		
17		18		
19		20		
21		22		

1. Display
2. Pig
3. Shop available for business
4. What you write with
5. Not the back
6. Place for baptism
7. Mad
8. Silly
9. Awareness of danger
10. A long way
11. A fish
12. Hat
13. Tidy
14. Device for catching fish
15. Wet
16. Unit of electrical current
17. Falling water
18. Was in the race
19. Someone who annoys
20. Domestic animal
21. Blow with axe
22. Policeman

LEVEL C

ANSWER NO.84

The letters below spell out six three-letter words. The letters of each word are in different type styles but always in the same order. The order is this

A B *C*

A *D* N *T*
D

D **E** A *D*

B **N** A
A *T* *D*
B **E** A

A

PUZZLE 64

Find a four-letter word which can be added to the end of the words of the left-hand column and the beginning of the words in the right-hand column to give 10 new words.

BACK	BAG
BEFORE	BALL
FREE	BELL
LONG	BOOK
OFF	CUFF

PUZZLE 65

Re-arrange the letters in the grid to find the name of a computer game hero.

ANSWER NO.15

PUZZLE 66

Identify the animals and fish concealed among
the letters. The words may run in any direction and
may overlap.

T	A	B	E	A	R	G	S	G	A
P	C	O	D	F	O	T	S	H	B
A	G	O	T	R	Q	U	N	V	D
R	T	H	F	L	M	N	A	W	R
R	C	I	D	E	S	A	K	K	A
O	R	S	G	T	U	N	E	L	P
T	A	V	T	E	C	B	O	P	O
U	G	Z	Q	S	R	L	J	R	E
H	I	Y	E	K	N	O	M	E	L
C	E	L	E	P	H	A	N	T	D

LEVEL C

◆?◆ ANSWER NO.102 ◆?◆

PUZZLE 67

Find a word or name that goes with the one we have
given and then read down the first letter of each
answer. You should find a nameless word!

	pie
	conquest
	singer
	watchman
	fever
	Twain
	poppy
	duckling
	spray

◆ ? ◆ ANSWER NO.33 ◆ ? ◆

NAIL NIBBLERS

PUZZLE 68

The letters written on the petals contain anagrams of five common wild flowers. Can you name them?

RIMSO REP

SAYID

PTUTB UCRE

LULBE EBL

HRTA EEH

◇?◇ ANSWER NO.128 ◇?◇

PUZZLE 69

Below you'll find a list of words containing 'E' as their only vowel. Can you locate them in the big 'E' shape? Which is the word that appears twice?

BEETLE	HERE	PEPPER
CEMETERY	JESTER	REFEREE
CLEVER	KESTREL	REFERENCE
CRESCENT	LETTER	SEETHE
DETERGENT	MEDLEY	THEME
EFFECT	MESSENGER	TEPEE
ENTENTE	MERGE	VESSEL
FERMENT	METHYLENE	WHEREVER
GREENERY	NEEDLE	YEN
HELMET	NETTLES	

```
M Y R E F E R E N C E N R Y R R K E
E E N V E S E R E V E R E H W W E S
S N E C E F F E C T Y M T E S S S E
Y T E E G E R F L S E E T E N N R S
R S D N R K E R E H S F E D B B N P
E E L S E R J E T E F E L T H H Y E
N J E S M R E
E H T E E S Y
E E N T J E T B Y F L E C H T E K R
R T P N Y E E R F E S E L T T E N E
G R E E T P M T E P L G E N E R E P
F R E G N E S S E M R D V E V C F P
E V T R E T L E T E M L E E H R F E
E E N E C P R R E M S E R L M Y R P
L Y K T S P E
C R R E E K H
V E E D R E C E B E V G Y F E E R I
E T T F C S E E N E L Y H T E M H E
T E S S E T F L S M E T S E C S E M
E M E E F R F S T E S T E M L E H E
N E J R B E E T R E F E L X J V E H
T C E C R L M E T N E T N E E N E T
```

LEVEL C

◇ ? ◇ ANSWER NO. 145 ◇ ? ◇

PUZZLE 70

Solve the clues and you will find that the first letter of
the answers make a word when read down.
Clue: May be shocking.

Clue	Answer
Natural force	
Greater in length	
Live coal	
British sport	
Medicine in pill form	
Herb with girl's name	
Herb found in pizza	
Walk slowly	
Never-ending	

ANSWER NO.164

PUZZLE 71

When you solve these clues and fill the answers
into the grid you will find that it reads the same down
and across.

1. **Not slow.**

2. **A particular piece of ground.**

3. **In a tennis match there are a maximum of five.**

4. **A piece of work to be done.**

◆ ? ◆ ANSWER NO.24 ◆ ? ◆

PUZZLE 72

The new postman has been given an important parcel to deliver to the house of Pearl Precious, the movie star. He doesn't know the exact number of the house but the guys at the sorting office have given him a few clues. See if you can help him to find the right house.

1. Pearl Precious has no pets.

2. The number of her house cannot be divided by 3.

3. Pearl does not have milk delivered.

4. Pearl hates flowers.

5. The number of the house is not a prime number.

? ANSWER NO. 42 ?

PUZZLE 73

Put a word in the middle space which makes,
when added to the end of the words on the left and
the beginning of the words on the right, eight new
eight-letter words.

BARE		ACHE
COME		HAND
DRAW		BONE
FEED		DROP

ANSWER NO.77

PUZZLE 74

Take a letter from each cloud in turn and make four
words connected with bad weather.

ANSWER NO.95

PUZZLE 75

When you have solved all the clues, read the first letter of the answers and you will find a hidden word. The clue is a mystery.

Clue	Answer
Violet	
Quantity	
Agreement	
Athletic competition	
Sub-continent	
Adhesive	
Wet weather gear	
Pachyderm	

LEVEL C

❬?❭ ANSWER NO.6 ❬?❭

PUZZLE 76

The diagram shows the front of a very clever type of safe. Turn each wheel in the order given and you will be able to open the door. What is the proper order?

 appears here but represents the N-W-E-S compass indicator.

The final square is to the south of the square two places east of the square which is one place due south of the square at the extreme north west.

 represents the 3×3 grid of lettered wheels: A D G / B E H / C F I.

NAIL NIBBLERS

 ⟨?⟩ ANSWER NO.121 ⟨?⟩

PUZZLE 77

Eight kids are hiding in the grid below hoping to avoid school. Their names are: PETE, SUSIE, DICK, MICHELLE, JOSH, HOLLY, LARRY, and JULIA. Can you find them? The names may be spelt in any direction, not necessarily in a straight line.

J	H	A	C	D	J	U	L	V	Q
O	S	R	T	S	U	L	N	I	P
A	P	V	D	N	E	S	I	E	A
N	E	W	K	I	P	Q	U	R	H
C	T	E	L	J	C	S	O	G	T
Y	Q	T	E	I	U	K	Z	X	C
R	E	L	L	E	H	C	I	M	R
R	V	A	K	L	T	E	B	O	J
A	T	U	H	O	L	L	Y	Y	S
L	K	L	H	O	P	R	U	T	G

LEVEL C

ANSWER NO.138

PUZZLE 78

The following sentences have been written in a special
way to hide their meaning. If you look at them
carefully you may get the message.

RGELA HANTSELEP DOMSEL KLWA CKLYQUI

TERSHAMS ERNEV KETA NCHLU THWI DILESCROCO

ENEV LLSMA FFESGIRA EPSLE DINGSTAN

IFULBEAUT RFLIESBUTTE TERFLIT ONGAM WERSFLO

ANTGI DASPAN ELLDW ONGAM BOOBAM VESGRO

ANSWER NO.171

PUZZLE 79

The following are books in which the words have been jumbled. Can you sort them out?

CENTRE THE TO EARTH OF JOURNEY TO

THE OF MOHICANS LAST THE

SERVICE HER SECRET MAJESTY'S ON

PRAIRIE THE HOUSE LITTLE THE ON

THOUSAND SEA UNDER LEAGUES TWENTY THE

ANSWER NO.67

PUZZLE 80

When you have solved the clues you will find that the
first letter of the answers will give a hidden word
reading down.

Instrument for giving commands	
Assault	
Fighting vehicle	
Strategy	
Not yet a captain	
Foe	

NAIL NIBBLERS

Clue: Part of a war

ANSWER NO.154

PUZZLE 81

The jumbled words in the bubbles are all languages.
How many can you unscramble?

ANSWER NO. 50

LEVEL C

PUZZLE 82

The letters on the side of the glue pot make the word
adhesives. How many words of four letters or more
can you make out of the nine letters given?

A V E
D S I
H E S

NAIL NIBBLERS

ANSWER NO.59

PUZZLE 83

The answer to each line becomes part of the clue to the next one. What are the seven words?

The first word is good to spend;

Change the first letter for something to eat;

Add a letter in front for a sham;

Drop the last letter to have a long-distance chat;

Drop the first letter, change the third for where you live;

Change the third but don't fall in this;

Change the first letter to leave you with a burrowing animal.

ANSWER NO.85

PUZZLE 84

The words below have had letters replaced by playing card symbols. Each symbol always stands for the same letter. Can you work out what the words should be? We have given some clues to help.

BU ♥♥♠♦   yellow spread

♥O♥♥♠♦   unsteady walk

BA♦♦♠♣   contains water?

♣ONGA♠♦   increased length

♦UBB♣♠   broken stones

♥O♥A♣S   sums

NAIL NIBBLERS

This fairy tale character became confused after failing to recognise her grandmother. Can you sort her out?

EIGHT TENDRIL IDOL ROD

LEVEL C

PUZZLE 86

The sentences below conceal the names of countries.
All the letters are in the right order.

The names are well hidden,
mark my words!

I can adamantly state you will
not find them.

It will anger many of you to
search in vain.

But do not let your ire land
you in trouble.

Attack the problem with new
zeal and overcome it.

ANSWER NO.103

PUZZLE 87

The answer to each line becomes part of the clue to
the next one. What are the seven words?

The first word has already been said;

Remove the third letter for a
clenched hand;

Jumble the letters to put through a sieve;

Change the first to raise weights in sport
and body building;

Jumble the letters to fly from here
to there;

Remove the second to be in
good shape;

Change the last for an
edible fruit.

LEVEL C

PUZZLE 88

Each of the groups of words below has an odd one
out. Can you find them all?

CHEESE
MILK
BUTTER
EGGS

JANUARY
SEPTEMBER
AUGUST
DECEMBER

SPIDER
ANT
CRICKET
BUTTERFLY

ENGLAND
SPAIN
GREECE
POLAND

CALIFORNIA
UTAH
TEXAS
NOVA SCOTIA

JAGUAR
LINCOLN
HARLEY-
DAVIDSON
PORSCHE

GANGES
THAMES
MISSISSIPPI
CAMBRIDGE

CUMULUS
NIMBUS
CYCLONE
STRATUS

NAIL NIBBLERS

◆ ANSWER NO.32 ◆

PUZZLE 89

Below are ten clues. To help you solve them,
we've supplied the vowels for each answer.

1. To turn about on a axis   `_ O _ A _ E`

2. Juicy   `_ U _ _ U _ E _`

3. Helps after dinner   `_ I _ _ A _ E`

4. Unfriendly   `_ O _ I _ E`

5. Of the night   `_ O _ U _ A _`

6. A border between two countries   `_ _ O _ I E`

7. To tear roughly   `_ A _ E _ A _ E`

8. To unroll a flag   `U _ _ U _`

9. To have an unjust opinion of   `_ I _ _ U _ E`

10. Four times a year   `_ U A _ _ E _ _`

LEVEL C

ANSWER NO.129

PUZZLE 90

Below you'll find a list of rock and pop stars. All of them, except one, can be found hidden in the word search. Which one is missing? The names you have to find may be written forwards, backwards, upwards, downwards or diagonally.

Alexander O'Neal
Amy Grant
Belinda Carlisle
Billy Joel
Bobby Brown
Bon Jovi
Bruce Springsteen
Cathy Dennis
Cher
Debbie Gibson
En Vogue
Heart
Jade
Janet Jackson

Madonna
Mariah Carey
Martika
Michael Jackson
New Kids on the
Block
Prince
REM
Richard Marx
Right Said Fred
Take That
Whitney Houston
Wilson Philips

LEVEL C

```
D A M E G O N O S B I G E I B B E D O I
A Y I D U T T S P R I N G W H C A M S L
X O C G O H A N N O D A M R N A K O L L
M C H H D G K D A J B U N I Y T I D A J
I S A P E I E U P R I R R G E Z T E E D
N P E W O R T V E I G P E H R I R L N E
O I L S P Y H I E D F Y O T A R A L O L
T L J N I R A F A O A D M S C P M I R S
S L A O T N T I T Z G J V A H M X B E I
U I C B E E N V O G U E U I A E E K D L
O H K C O L B E H T N O S D I K W E N R
H P S D S O C E D A B E S F R A K E A A
Y N O A S O A R I Y F A N R A R C H X C
E O N J R R I Z E R H N O E M A A C E A
N S C E T V A Y A M E T D D V T J N L D
T L E R O N X R A M D R A H C I R I A N
I I Q J N E W K P H I L M C A K T B L I
H W N E E T S G N I R P S E C U R B A L
W O J B O B B Y B R O W N H A M E N P E
B E Q U I V A R K L P L E O J Y L L I B
```

◆ ANSWER NO163. ◆

PUZZLE 91

The words of these famous proverbs have been jumbled up. Can you unravel them?

1 Lady never won fair faint heart.

2 The bush is worth in the two hand in a bird.

3 No spilt crying it's milk use over.

4 Glass shouldn't live in stones houses who throw people.

NAIL NIBBLERS

ANSWER NO.23

PUZZLE 92

Try to find out the name of this fairy tale character.
Come to think of it, that was the point of the story!

ANSWER NO.41

PUZZLE 93

These film titles are written without vowels. Your task is to find the missing vowels and reveal the film.

1. TH WZRD F Z
2. CLS NCNTRS F TH THRD KND
3. PLLYNN
4. BCK T TH FTR
5. NTNL VLVT
6. BTMN RTRNS
7. BTY ND TH BST
8. HNY SHRNK TH KDS
9. TH SND F MSC
10. JRSSC PRK

ANSWER NO.176

PUZZLE 94

By moving one square up, down, right or left – not diagonally – follow the trail of letters in the grid and you will find the title of a Steven Spielberg film. But beware, there are six dummy letters included.

T	A	R	K	A
S	E	A	A	R
O	F	O	I	D
L	T	S	R	E
E	H	S	E	R

LEVEL C

PUZZLE 95

This kid stayed out late and lost her footing. Can you unscramble her and give the tale a happy ending?

ANSWER NO.5

PUZZLE 96

The words below spell out four well-known phrases.
The first word of each line is in the right place but the
others have been mixed up so that, although the word
is in the right place within a line, it has been moved
up or down and is now in the wrong line. You
have to sort them out. To help you there is a
clue for each line.

Here	big	the	she	and	grand	bush
What	lion	eyes	you	lost	her	wardrobe
The	Bo	go	witch	have	mulberry	sheep
Little	we	Peep	round	the	the	mama

Clues: Line 1. Nursery Rhyme

Line 2. Little Red Riding Hood

Line 3. Narnia

Line 4. Careless Shepherdess

LEVEL C

Can you decipher these film titles?

1 Excellent and Adventure Ted's Bill.

2 Eighty in Around Days World the.

3 of Purple Cairo The Rose.

4 an Stepmother My Alien is.

5 Being Importance The Earnest of.

NAIL NIBBLERS

ANSWER NO.137

PUZZLE 98

The following proverbs have been rewritten using a long word or words where a short one would have been better! See if you can work out what we mean.

1. It is a malicious shift of atmospheric pressure which fails to produce benefits for some members of the population.

2. A surfeit of hard labour unmixed with recreational activities has the unfortunate effect of making Jack a rather uninteresting youth.

3. An excessive number of culinary operatives tends to have an extremely adverse effect upon the quality of the pottage.

4. It is said to be impossible to fabricate a money-holding device of fine cloth from the aural appendage of a porcine quadruped.

5. When precipitation occurs it has a marked tendency to do so in excessive quantities.

LEVEL C

? ANSWER NO. 172 ?

PUZZLE 99

How well do you know stage musicals, old and new?
Below you'll find some of them with their vowels
missing. Can you work out what the musicals
should be?

1. PHNTM F TH PR
2. CRSL
3. VT
4. STRLGHT XPRSS
5. TH SND F MSC
6. LS MSRBLS
7. CHSS
8. MSS SGN
9. RCKY HRRR SHW
10. CTS

NAIL NIBBLERS

PUZZLE 100

This fairy tale character was a bit of a bird brain.
Maybe that's how she got so confused.

LEVEL C

ANSWER NO.155

PUZZLE 101

Can you find the ten movies hidden in the passage below?

I often visit my cousin on a Friday afternoon. On this particular occasion she was doodling on a piece of green card when I arrived. I couldn't be sure (she's not exactly famous for her artistic talents!) but her drawing seemed to be of a group of gorillas. In the mist outside her window I could just make out her dog frolicking in the flowerbeds.

As was her custom, my cousin made me a cup of tea. I don't know about you, but I can't drink tea until it's cooled off a bit. Some like it hot, but I'm certainly not one of them!

"Who's that girl?" I inquired, pointing at a photograph that was perched on top of her television.

"That's Hannah – and her sisters are in the other photo over there. Hannah's a mannequin – it's a wonderful life for her, you know. In the world of fashion modelling she's a real star.

Wars may happen, natural disasters change the face of the earth as we know it, but Hannah will always be a success. By contrast, her sisters do little – women, they believe, shouldn't leave the kitchen sink."

ANSWER NO.49

PUZZLE 102

The words below spell out four well-known phrases. The first word of each line is in the right place but the others have been mixed up so that, although the word is in the right place within a line, it has been moved up or down and is now in the wrong line. You have to sort them out. To help you there is a clue for each line.

The	does	and	Pooh	king
The	huff	at	future	puff
How	house	your	I'll	Corner
I'll	once	and	garden	grow

Clues: Line 1. King Arthur

Line 2. Christopher Robin

Line 3. Contrary Gardener

Line 4. Big Bad threat

LEVEL C

◆?◆ ANSWER NO.58 ◆?◆

PUZZLE 103

The following are well-known books disguised in newspaper headlines.

GIRL IN RABBIT HOLE DRAMA CLAIMS BIZARRE ADVENTURE

SMALL BOY IN MOUSE TRANSFORMATION. SHOCKING WITCHCRAFT ALLEGATION

MISSISSIPPI BOY — PRESUMED DEAD — RETURNS WITH TREASURE

TRANSYLVANIAN COUNT WANTED ON ASSAULT CHARGES FLEES TO ENGLAND

MARINER CLAIMS STRANGE ADVENTURE AMONG TINY PEOPLE

NAIL NIBBLERS

◆ ANSWER NO. 86 ◆

PUZZLE 104

Here are some more proverbs disguised with pompous phrasing and long words. Simplify!

1. Everything which reflects sparkling brilliance is not necessarily composed of a precious, malleable, ductile metallic element.

2. A concretion of mineral matter incessantly turning upon its surface is extremely unlikely to acquire a collection of small primitive plants.

3. Herbage always appears to have a more intense shade of verdancy when it is seen upon the far side of a boundary marker.

4. In order to apprehend someone who misappropriates the property of others it is necessary to retain the services of a person engaged in the same profession.

5. It is a strange fact that vexatious circumstances always appear to arrive as triplets.

ANSWER NO. 111

PUZZLE 105

Can you work out what these proverbs are supposed to be? One word of each proverb can be found in each column.

Too	stitch	rains	but	it	day
A	many	built	feather	a	broth
It	wasn't	cooks	in	flock	pours
Rome	of	a	time	saves	together
Birds	never	in	spoil	the	nine

ANSWER NO.13

PUZZLE 106

Here are some book titles in which all the consonants have been removed. Can you work out the titles just from the vowels? It's rather difficult, so we've given a clue to each one.

1. `[ O | I | O ] [ U | O E ]`
2. `[ I ] [ A | I ] [ O | I | O N ]`
3. `[ E ] [ E E ] [ U | E E ]`
4. `[ A E ] [ O ] [ O ] [ O | A | I ]`
5. `[ E ] [ O | I | E ] [ O ] [ A | I A ]`

1. Desert Island.

2. Another island, same name!

3. All for one!

4. Hobbit friend

5. Aslan

ANSWER NO.104

LEVEL C

PUZZLE 107

What is the musical instrument hidden in the riddle?

My first is in PROMISE, but not in PRIZE

My second's in ACTOR, but not COMPROMISE

My third is in EXCELLENCE, but not in OVER

My fourth is in ORANGE, and also in CLOVER

My fifth is in SLOPE, but not in GREASE

My sixth is in SHELF, but not in PEACE

My seventh's in POLITE, and also in POINT

My eighth is in TONGUE, and also ANOINT

My ninth is in GRAPE, but not in GONG

And here is the end of my silly song!

ANSWER NO.130

PUZZLE 108

The words on the scales of the monster are an anagram of a dinosaur name though, needless to say, it is not the one pictured. Can you work out which big beast is hidden in the puzzle?

ANSWER NO.31

HEAD BANGERS

★ LEVEL D ★

PUZZLE 109

If you add the same letter to the end of the left word
and the start of the right one on each line, you will
find the name of a famous film star reading down.
Who is he?

	?	
STAR	?	WINE
CELL	?	MISSION
FAR	?	ASK
AMNESIA	?	REST
ANGLE	?	AFTER
MEN	?	NIT
CHILL	?	SLAM
TUB	?	HOE
SHIN	?	BONY

◆? ANSWER NO.147 ?◆

PUZZLE 110

My first is in TIGER, but not in CAT

My second's in UGLY, but not
ACROBAT

My next is in UMBRELLA, and also
in BELL

My fourth is in OWL, but not
in JEWEL

My fifth and my fourth are two peas
in a pod

My whole is a dwelling that some
may find odd

LEVEL D

? ANSWER NO.162 ?

PUZZLE 111

The names of three creatures often found as pets have been mixed up. All the letters are in the right order.

D G O
O
R A G
L
D B B
F
I I T S
H

ANSWER NO.22

PUZZLE 112

The following figures, representing certain letters, make up a ten letter word:

1   2   3   4   5   6   7   8   9   10

Your task is to work out the above word by making use of the clues below.

 means a list specifying a fixed order

 means part of the nose

 means a lion's home

 means combat on horseback

ANSWER NO.40

PUZZLE 113

Below you'll find the names of five birds which all
start from the central C. The letters which make up
the words are connected vertically, horizontally and
diagonally. Not every letter is used and some may be
used more than once. What are the birds?

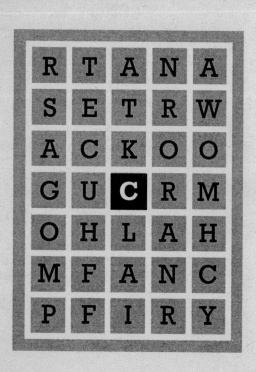

ANSWER NO. 75

PUZZLE 114

The unpronounceable jumbles below are really States in America without their vowels. How many of them can you unravel?

CLFRN

DH

NBRSK

HW

LSK

◆?◆ ANSWER NO.93 ◆?◆

PUZZLE 115

All the words in the left-hand box have something in common. Which of the words in the right-hand box should join them?

DRAPERY	SPEND
COWARD	SAUCER
SPIGOT	CATAPULT
DOGGED	BICYCLE

ANSWER NO. 119

PUZZLE 116

All the answers to the clues below are five-letter words. When you have written them in the grid, you will be able to read the names of two signs of the zodiac down the first and last columns. Which ones?

LEVEL D

1. To move around quietly

2. Someone who says you were with them when the crime was committed.

3. You have these on fingers and toes.

4. Man who makes you laugh as his job.

5. Bird of prey.

6. A train runs on these.

◇❬?❭ ANSWER NO.4 ❬?❭◇

PUZZLE 117

Below are ten clues. To help you we've supplied the
consonants for each answer.

1. Not straightforward

| | B | L | | Q | | |

2. The unlimited extent of space

| | N | F | | N | | T | Y |

3. Conceit

| | R | R | | G | | N | C | |

4. To recover after sickness

| C | | N | V | | L | | S | C | |

5. A period of 1000 years

| M | | L | L | | N | N | | | M |

6. Having effects below the level of conscious awareness

| S | | B | L | | M | | N | | L |

7. Having human characteristics

| H | | M | | N | | D |

8. Inventiveness

| | N | G | | N | | | T | Y |

9. Basic

| R | | D | | M | | N | T | | R | Y |

10. A bunch of flowers

| B | | | Q | | | T |

◆ ANSWER NO.136 ◆

PUZZLE 118

As you can see, a shark has been at work. He's chewed up a lot of fish and left their spare syllables scattered on the sea bed. However, you may be able to save the situation by putting the syllables back together again to form the names of five kinds of fish. Which is the one left over?

DUCK

HAD CU DA

BAR

CAT

DOCK

BOM

FISH

PIR

AN HA

BEL

RA BAY

LEVEL D

ANSWER NO. 173

PUZZLE 119

Here are 40 sets of three letters. Using each set only once and without changing the order of the letters can you make 20 six-letter English words?

ora	suf	ver	ral
gin	ang	por	did
pen	bas	ear	ous
mal	nor	lay	wig
can	fam	plu	try
sen	sel	law	ter
out	mis	ket	dam
dle	ius	gen	age
joc	qua	hap	key
fix	voy	cud	mar

ANSWER NO.48

PUZZLE 120

Can you find a nine-letter word scrambled in the
square? Clue: A bit jumpy.

PUZZLE 121

Your first task is to solve the clues below. When you
have your seven answers, you'll find these letters also
contain the names of five breeds of dog.
Which breeds?

CLUES

GREAT JOY AND HIGH SPIRITS	_ _ _ _ _ _ _
EVERYTHING	_ _ _
A PIECE OF INCLINED GROUND	_ _ _ _ _
SPAGHETTI IS AN EXAMPLE OF THIS	_ _ _ _ _
HUE OFTEN ASSOCIATED WITH ROSES	_ _ _
TO MAKE SOMEONE A PRIEST	_ _ _ _ _ _
AN OBJECT WHICH SEPARATES	_ _ _ _ _ _ _

ANSWER NO.156

PUZZLE 122

Each line in the rhyme below gives one letter of a well-known city. Can you work out the identity of this ten-letter European capital?

My first is in TRACE, but not in PLAN

My second's in ROTTEN, but not in MILAN

My third is in PORTRAIT, but not in SUNRISE

My fourth is in PRETTY, and also SURPRISE

My fifth is in FRIEND, but not in COMPARE

My sixth is in GHETTO, but not in DESPAIR

My seventh's in DECADE, and also in DAMP

My eighth is in GINGER, but not in REVAMP

My ninth is in GOVERN, and also in NIECE

My tenth is in LANGUAGE, but is not
in CEASE.

LEVEL D

? ANSWER NO.57 ?

PUZZLE 123

How may words of three letters or more can you find
in this square? The computer found 102, but as you
don't have a microchip in your head we don't expect
you to get quite so many! A score of fifteen is good,
twenty-five very good and forty or more excellent.
What is the nine letter word?

ANSWER NO.87

PUZZLE 124

Which of the following can be seen at some time in the night sky, with a telescope if necessary?

URSA MAJOR   BETELGEUSE

ORION   COPERNICUS

CUMULUS   ANTARCTICA

HORSE NEBULA   PLUTO

JOHN MAJOR   CASCARA

NEPTUNE   PERSEIDS

VENUS   HALLEY'S COMET

HADES   DOMESTICA

LEVEL D

ANSWER NO.110

PUZZLE 125

Below you'll find some anagrams of well-known people. Can you work out who they are?

1. **G's huge bore**
   (American politician)

2. **C Kindles Search**
   (English writer)

3. **Moodier Me**
   (Actress)

4. **Shy without neon**
   (Singer)

5. **A new antic – So?**
   (Inventor)

ANSWER NO.12

PUZZLE 126

Take a letter from each country in turn to make
another 7 letter country. Clue: It could feel a little
chilly here!

I R E L A N D

A M E R I C A

G E R M A N Y

F I N L A N D

A U S T R I A

D E N M A R K

E N G L A N D

PUZZLE 127

Look carefully at the following 'words'. If you replace the numbers with Roman numerals you should be able to read them easily.

1000 o 500 1 100 u 1000

100 a 500 1000 1 u 1000

a 100 a 500 e 1000 1 100

500 u 1000 1000 1 e 500

a 100 100 e 500 e 500

ANSWER NO.131

PUZZLE 128

Reading down, the name of a well-known young actress should be revealed in the middle column which is currently empty. To discover her identity, it is useful for you to know that each letter of her name will help you create two brand new words on every line, the left one ending with the letter, the right one starting.

Who is she?

HALLO		ASH
SCAMP		DEAL
AWAKE		EON
CAME		WE
ARISE		OR
ARE		KIN
PEA		EACH
BUS		OWL
JOSTLE		ARK
HOP		VENT
STRANGE		ANKLE

LEVEL D

ANSWER NO.30

PUZZLE 129

The jumble of letters below contains five three-letter words. Each is the name of a living creature. The letters are in different type styles but always in the same order. The order is:

A B C

T
A N R D T
T
A
C
A T A B G O

ANSWER NO. 148

PUZZLE 130

There are five five-letter words hidden in the light
bulbs. Take a letter from each bulb to find them.
They have all something to do with light.

ANSWER NO. 161

PUZZLE 131

If you cut letters in half horizontally it is much easier
to recognise the top half than the bottom. For that
reason all the words below are made up from – you
guessed! – bottom halves. To help you, all the words
are types of food.

PIZZA

CHICKEN

DOUGHNUT

SANDWICH

SALAD

ICE CREAM

ANSWER NO.21

PUZZLE 132

The names of two animals are hidden in each of the sentences below. Can you find them?

1. A dynamo used by a mad scientist will endanger billionaires.

2. On her job application form she epitomised all the qualities they required.

3. Noah's tendency to cherish arks was perfectly understandable.

4. William wants to grab bits of gossip like him, do you abhor secrecy.

5. Peering through the uncommon keyhole he learnt of plans of their brilliant elopement.

6. He would like to go to Moscow but she insists on Budapest.

7. His bravado gave us a false impression: indeed the whole thing's a sham, sternness being our best reaction.

8. I prefer athletics, although the commentator's waffle annoys me.

LEVEL D

◆? ANSWER NO.39 ?◆

PUZZLE 133

Below you can see a number of syllables in alphabetical order and a list of clues. All the answers to the clues can be made from combinations of the syllables given. Each syllable is used ONCE only. When you have solved all the clues, the first letters should give you the name of a well-known fictional character.

A	AL	AP	BRA	DI	DOUG	EM	GE	GO	IN	IT
JE	LA	LAS	LE	LEM	LY	MARE	MI	NA	NEP	NIGHT
ON	OR	OS	PER	PLE	PO	RU	SA	SA	TRICH	TUNE

CLUES

EUROPEAN COUNTRY (5)

FRENCH EMPEROR (8)

BOY'S NAME (6)

COLOUR OF THE RAINBOW (6)

FRUIT (5)

DREAM (9)

BRANCH OF MATHEMATICS (7)

HOLY CITY (9)

FLIGHTLESS BIRD (7)

PLANET (7)

SUPREME RULER (7)

SAUSAGE (6)

ANSWER NO.92

PUZZLE 134

The grid contains some letters to help you. Use the
clues to fill in the missing letters and you will find a
word written along the body of the snake.

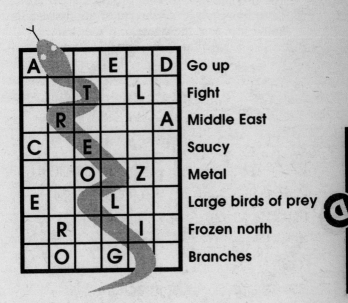

A		E		D

Go up

Fight

Middle East

Saucy

Metal

Large birds of prey

Frozen north

Branches

PUZZLE 135

The leaves of the tree contain groups of letters which, when unscrambled, will give you the names of five types of tree. What are they?

ANSWER NO.118

PUZZLE 136

Look at the words on this moon map.
They form an anagram of a well known lunar feature.

ANSWER NO.135

PUZZLE 137

In each sentence you'll find the name of one sport hidden. Can you locate all six of them?

1. The whole thing was rather a shock, eyebrows being raised in the highest of places.

2. The English aristocracy clings to old values, for it fears a world without them.

3. That really was a bad mint on the whole; it stuck to my teeth like glue.

4. Her horrid ingratitude was beyond belief, and she was sent to bed without supper.

5. My cat will attack a rat every time.

6. He started making loud jokes in order to mask a tingling in his left foot.

ANSWER NO.157

PUZZLE 138

Danny Diablo has gone on a school outing to the art gallery. His teacher prayed that, for once, he would be good but within minutes of entering the building he has switched round the names of several famous artists. Can you rearrange them before the warder notices and throws the whole class out?

VINCENT   CHAGALL

LEONARDO   PICASSO

PABLO   CONSTABLE

JOHN   DA VINCI

MARC   VAN GOGH

LEVEL D

ANSWER NO.174

PUZZLE 139

The words below have some of their letters replaced by symbols. Each symbol always represents the same letter. To help you we have also put in some clues.

✿ ■ ◗ ☎ ✈ ◗

Trading before money

✿ ■ ♥ ♥ ✓ ✓ N

Party wind bag

C ◗ ✈ ■ ☎ ✈

Make

☎ ◗ ■ D ✈ ◗

Dealer

♥ ✓ ✓ ☎ ✈ ◗

Plunderer

✿ ✈ ◗ ■ ☎ ✈

Scold harshly

‹? ANSWER NO.70 ?›

PUZZLE 140

Along the arms of the tentacles of the octopus you will see the names of marine creatures disguised in a special way. How many can you catch?

ANSWER NO.47

TEETH GRINDERS

★ LEVEL E ★

PUZZLE 141

The seven letter words below are all in code. The same symbol always stands for the same letter. To help you a clue is given at the end of each line and two letters have been left uncoded.

✳ ☆ ◻ ◆ ✏ ✹ ♥ Mistake

✳ R ❄ ▼ ● ◆ ✏ Robber

● ◻ ✏ ❄ B ☆ ✹ Heard

♥ ✹ ✳ ▲ ◻ ◆ ✏ Recoil

▼ ● ♥ ✳ ☆ ✹ ✏ Confused

◆ ? ◆ ANSWER NO.56 ◆ ? ◆

PUZZLE 142

The following sentence is missing three words which are anagrams of each other. Each dash represents a missing letter. What are the words?

The _ _ _ _ _ _ said that

I was a _ _ _ _ _ _ _

because I had the word

_ _ _ _ _ _ written

on my hand in the

spelling test.

PUZZLE 143

The answers to the clues below can be found in the list of syllables. However, all the syllables have been presented in alphabetical order. See if you can rearrange them.

BI	CATH	CLE	COM	CY	ED	FISH	GA	GOLD	MA
NAI	OS	PIZ	PU	RAL	SI	TER	TRICH	ZA	ZINE

CLUES
1. INFORMATION PROCESSOR
2. WILDERNESS AREA SOUTH OF ISRAEL
3. LARGE CHURCH
4. ITALIAN OPEN PIE
5. AQUATIC PET
6. LARGE FLIGHTLESS BIRD
7. PERIODICAL
8. CONVEYANCE

ANSWER NO. 109

PUZZLE 144

The following eight-letter words have been coded
using Greek style letters. Even if you don't know any
Greek you will be able to work out the words
if you use the clues we have given.

Λ Ξ Φ Γ Λ Μ Ε Τ

HANDBONES

Δ Φ Γ Λ Μ Ι Ξ Η

BABY DUCK

Ι Ξ Λ Μ Ι Ξ Η Τ

VAGUE IDEAS

Π Ι Γ Λ Μ Ι Ξ Η

PRESERVING FOOD

Ι Ξ Γ Μ Φ Δ Ε Τ

CONTAINS

LEVEL E

◆ ANSWER NO.11 ◆

PUZZLE 145

The following sentences have been de-punctuated to turn them into nonsense. Can you add punctuation to make them grammatical? Each is not necessarily a single sentence.

1. She said that that that that I said should have been those

2. The culprit made his admission sorrowfully the day after he was shot

3. I said and but he said I said but but he was wrong and I said so

TEETH GRINDERS

ANSWER NO.106

PUZZLE 146

The words in the box have something in common.
Which of the following words should join them?

cup
group
proud
buds
jogs

?

kill

then

bugs

LEVEL E

E

ANSWER NO.132

PUZZLE 147

The following groups of words are all proverbs in
which the wordshave been jumbled up.
How many can you work out?

1 And many between cup
there's slip a lip

2 They count before your
hatch chickens don't

3 Judge cover by its never
a book

4 Most vessels make
empty noise

5 Be out find your sure sin
will you

ANSWER NO.29

PUZZLE 148

A rebus is a word, phrase or saying cunningly hidden in a illustration. Here are a few to try.

◇?◇ ANSWER NO.149 ◇?◇

PUZZLE 149

The answers to the clues below are syllables which, when rearranged, will make the names of five countries. To help you, there's a hint to the identity of the syllables in brackets after each clue.

A stain or blot (rhymes with 'spark')

Me (rhymes with 'pie')

An old fashioned girl's name (rhymes with 'wader')

Home of a predatory animal (rhymes with 'when')

The first letter of the alphabet (rhymes with 'pay')

Some (rhymes with 'penny')

Part of the face (rhymes with 'bin')

A tin for food (rhymes with 'man')

Past tense of run (rhymes with 'fan')

Common name for the thing which causes illness (rhymes with 'worm')

E

ANSWER NO.160

PUZZLE 150

Can you fill in these blanks? In each puzzle the letters
missing are the same for every line.

ANSWER NO.20

PUZZLE 151

Using the letters we have given you and the clues on the right fill in the missing letters. When you have finished you will find there is a word running down the snake.

Finger

Thousands of Years

Desert plants

Hit

Tree Seed

Pains

Another name

Happiness

Greek Island

ANSWER NO.38

PUZZLE 152

Can you unravel these ten words? The clues in brackets could help you, as they mean the same as the scrambled words.

1. **EITDRVNE**
   (back to front)

2. **DAEOFHLSO**
   (lie)

3. **VLICARUSHO**
   (gallant)

4. **ASDEHFMI**
   (starving)

5. **HIANVS**
   (disappear)

6. **REOMET**
   (shooting star)

7. **LHEROCT**
   (laugh)

8. **UPSSEO**
   (husband)

9. **CARCIEP**
   (whim)

10. **ETRPMEITD**
    (allowed)

LEVEL E

◆?◆ ANSWER NO.73 ◆?◆

PUZZLE 153

The words in the box have been chosen according to a simple system. Can any of the words outside join them.

ape
eight
igloo
orange
umbrella

?

knowledge

garden

purple

ANSWER NO.91

PUZZLE 154

In each of the five sentences below two numbers are hiding. It is your task to seek them out.

1. Bridget went yesterday, anxious even though we had reassured her she would be alright.

2. At the windmill I once played my accordion every day.

3. Keith reeled in surprise as the horse's sudden neigh threw him into confusion.

4. He was left woefully short of cash, having been spending again in excess of what he could truly afford.

5. The scheme was foolproof, our accountant encouraged us to start immediately.

LEVEL E

? ANSWER NO.2 ?

PUZZLE 155

Use the clues to fill in the missing words and complete the snail. To help you you'll find that the last letter of each word must be used as the first letter of the next word. The number of letters for each answer is given at the end of the clue.

1. Pay this in class or teacher won't be pleased (9)

2. This is most of the air we breath (8)

3. Lump of gold (6)

4. You can bear it – just about! (9)

5. Weird (5)

6. Aubergine (8)

7. The hare will always beat him in the race (8)

8. The person who saw the crime (10)

9. A noisy quarrel (8)

10. Getting the chop at dawn! (9)

11. Zero (7)

ANSWER NO.117

PUZZLE 156

Take a letter from each animal and make five
six-letter words connected with farms.

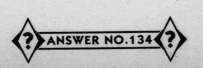

ANSWER NO.134

PUZZLE 157

Here we have mixed the names of trees with the names of places where people live. See if you can untangle the resulting strange words.

PALBEAM

MASTLE

HORNACE   CAPLE

GALOWRED

BUNWOOD

MONAR

COTTORY   HICKAGE

CEDASTERY

◆?◆ ANSWER NO. 175 ◆?◆

PUZZLE 158

The words around the circle can be rearranged to
form the name of a country.
Clue: 51

ADAMANT CERTIFIES TO USE

LEVEL E

PUZZLE 159

Complete the phrases below, then write the missing
words in the grid with the first letter in the box. You
should be able to read a six-letter word down.
Clue: Fish

_ _ _ **jump**

_ _ _ _ **site**

_ _ _ _ **storm**

_ _ _ _ _ **wave**

_ _ _ _ _ **days**

_ _ _ _ _ _ **badge**

TEETH GRINDERS E

PUZZLE 160

Change the top word into the bottom one by altering
a letter each time and forming a new word with
each move.

JOUST

PAINS

LEVEL E

CLOCK

BREAD

? ANSWER NO.46 ?

PUZZLE 161

Match the following words with their position on the body shown.

1. **Bridge**
2. **Crown**
3. **Temple**
4. **Lobe**
5. **Iris**
6. **Palm**
7. **Arch**
8. **Nape**

◆❓◆ ANSWER NO.55 ◆❓◆

PUZZLE 162

Below you will see thirty syllables. If you rearrange them you'll find that, using each syllable only once, they will make up ten three-syllable words. What are the words?

DI	VER	FLAB
SION	DI	IN
TIC	SUS	BU
MAN	PER	MEN
AB	RO	REAU
NEWS	TUDE	BER
TEER	CATE	CRAT
NANCE	VOL	DO
LON	GAST	UN
PA	GI	TE

PUZZLE 163

Use all the letters in the grid twice to give you two
nine-letter words.
The clue is: SILENT LADY KILLERS

TEETH GRINDERS

E

ANSWER NO.108

PUZZLE 164

The following clues will give you the name of six sports. Read the first letters of the words in order and you will be transported to Africa.

Natation	
Toxophily	
Soccer	
Track & Field	
Equestrianism	
Blade Balance	

ANSWER NO.10

PUZZLE 165

Which of the words in the right-hand column can join the left?

ABUNDANT	ELEPHANT
BLOATED	SARACEN
LEGGY	BLIZZARD
STEAM	SCORNED
SCREAMED	NEWT

ANSWER NO. 107

PUZZLE 166

Below you will find some clues. We have given you the answers as well! So where's the puzzle? Well, the answers have been broken into syllables arranged in alphabetical order. All you have to do is select the right syllables to answer each clue. Easy! Or is it?

1. AMERICAN UNIVERSITY

2. CAPITAL OF THAILAND

3. COMMON NAME OF PLANT RANUNCULUS

4. ANIMAL WHICH CARRIES ITS YOUNG IN A POUCH

5. GAMBLING GAME INVOLVING WHEEL

6. VERY HARD CRYSTALLINE CARBON

7. TREES WHICH LOOSE THEIR LEAVES IN WINTER

8. CALEDONIA

9. EATER OF ITS OWN KIND

10. PART OF OUR GALAXY

LEVEL E

A	AL	BANG	BUT	CAN	CUP	DEC	DI	ET
HAR	IAL	ID	KOK	LAND	LETTE	MAR	MOND	NIB
OUS	PLAN	ROU	SCOT	SUP	TER	U	VARD	

AAARGH!

★ **LEVEL F** ★

PUZZLE 167

The letters below can be fitted into the grid so that they give three words reading across and one down the middle.

P B T T F A Y C U S D E A N R A

1. Single letter vegetable 3. Well again

2. Nocturnal flying animal 4. Imagination

ANSWER NO. 28

PUZZLE 168

Five of the words below are related in some way.
Discover which ones they are and see if brass could
join them.

cease

hares

sloth

beach

again

brown

abbey

frown

green

beans

acids

drama

LEVEL F

? ANSWER NO.193 ?

PUZZLE 169

Turn the anagrams below into four classic works of English literature. Name the authors too. Clue: there is a hint to the theme of the books in the anagram.

1. MASK PLAN FIRED

2. SITED HARM

3. MAULED TO REJOIN

4. BOSS DEFILER V THE LUSTRE

AAARGH!

ANSWER NO.159

Look at the following list of words. There is something special about them. Can you work out what it is?

HOAX

THAW

ATOM

AVOW

IOTA

TAXI

MIAOW

LEVEL F

ANSWER NO.192

PUZZLE 171

Look at the signpost below. The distances given are related, by some form of twisted logic, to the place names. Can you work out the logic and then replace the question mark with the correct distance? If you want a clue, remember the words have consonants and vowels.

ANSWER NO.191

PUZZLE 172

The clues will help you to find ten hidden words all to
do with cycling. The words may be written in any
direction and the grid contains dummy letters.

A	X	M	I	R	R	O	R	H
B	E	L	D	D	A	S	B	A
W	I	L	R	T	V	E	S	N
P	O	C	E	T	L	S	E	D
E	E	U	Y	L	J	B	K	L
M	E	D	S	C	A	L	O	E
A	G	W	A	N	L	M	P	B
R	E	V	Q	L	R	E	S	A
F	N	I	A	H	C	T	Y	R
D	R	A	U	G	D	U	M	S

LEVEL F

1. Reflector
2. Steering
   device
3. Wheel parts
4. Foot rest
5. Driver
6. Splash
   preventor
7. Seat
8. Ringer
9. Bike
10. Skeleton

? ANSWER NO.37 ?

PUZZLE 173

ACROSS

1. Tall pole on a ship which supports the sail (4)
6. A person who has no parents (6)
8. Father (2)
9. Part of something (4)
10. It helps you to draw straight lines (5)
12. Tea, lemonade and orange juice are these (6)
13. To carry out something (2)
14. This would be steep to walk up (6)
16. A male deer (4)
18. You use this on your hair to make it stay in place (3)
19. A baby horse (4)
21. You open and close this (4)
23. A narrow passageway (8)

DOWN

1. The early part of the day (7)
2. I am, you _ _ _ (3)
3. A flash (5)
4. A type of bird (6)
5. An outlaw (6)
7. You use this to mend your clothes (6)
11. You fasten this in your hair to make it curl (6)
15. An eskimo's home (5)
16. Water in a plant (3)
17. As well (4)
19. A long way (3)
20. To unite by addition (3)
22. Either, _ _ (2)

AAARGH!

ANSWER NO.72

PUZZLE 174

The letters on the computer screen form a series.
What letter replaces the question mark?

OTTFF
SSEN?

ANSWER NO.90

LEVEL F

PUZZLE 175

Can you work out where these people live?
Fit the names correctly into the boxes and you should
have your answer!

4 letters
Andy
Mary
Mike
Paul

5 letters
Clare
Sarah
Tessa

6 letters
Amanda

7 letters
Mrs Hall
Shelley

9 letters
Catherine
Miss Cooke
Mr Bushell

11 letters
Miss Coomber
Mrs Tuckwell

◇ **ANSWER NO.1** ◇

PUZZLE 176

Five of the words below are related. Discover which ones they are and then see if confidence could join them.

encyclopedia

anteater
ahead
astrology
red
confederation
hopeless
acrimony
eagles
nausea
acids
telephone
sight
azalea

PUZZLE 177

The editor's going to be after me. A number puzzle in a word puzzle book! Whatever next? But no, I assure you this is a word puzzle. Why are some numbers above the line?

$$\frac{12 \qquad 6 \qquad 10}{345 \quad 789}$$

ANSWER NO.184

PUZZLE 178

Here is part of the menu from Joe's Diner. Joe has his own way of calculating the prices. We're not giving away too many secrets if we tell you it has someting to do with the position of letters in the alphabet. How much does Pizza cost? If you can work it out Joe will give you a free slice.

Joe's Diner

Hamburger	...... $9.30
Cheeseburger	......$11.60
Hot Dog	...... $6.90
Pizza	...... ?

ANSWER NO.189

PUZZLE 179

Your task here is to work out which letter of the alphabet is represented by each of the numbers 1 to 26. To help you, we've given you a few letters to start you off. When you work out what the numbers represent, write them in the reference grid at the bottom. The completed puzzle will look like a filled-in crossword, featuring only genuine words.

		8			22	16	10	6	4	7	4	3
25	8	11	11	6		8		16		21	7	
7		7		16		10			14		21	11
26	7	4	21		1		22	24	15	11		23
7			7		4	11			7			9
4			18	16	16		9	6	22	5		6
9	20	24	11		26				13	9	6	
	11			10	9	2	5	6		12		16
	8		2	7	6	11			17	11	7	20
			21		10	7	9	24				20
7	4	6		11		6			15		9	
	7		16			24		12	11	25	6	
	19	15	10	2	24	11				16		

1	2	3	4 R	5	6 T	7	8 W	9	10	11 E	12	13
14	15	16 O	17	18	19	20	21	22	23	24 L	25	26

LEVEL F

ANSWER NO.76

PUZZLE 180

Start at the top left corner and fill in the answers to the clues, working round the grid in a spiral. The last two letters of each answer form the first two of the next. The number of letters in each answer is given in brackets after the clue.

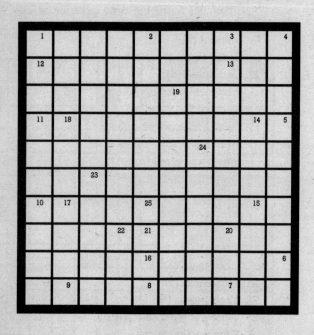

1. Capital of UK (6)
2. Vegetable (5)
3. One time only (4)
4. Stop completely (5)
5. Quite a few (7)
6. Permit (5)
7. Possessor (5)
8. Rub out (5)
9. Older (6)
10. Command (5)
11. Historical periods (4)
12. Study of the stars (9)
13. Gold, Frankincense and – – – – – (5)
14. Words with similar endings
    (eg. Prime time) (5)
15. Given by the Doctor (8)
16. Uneasy (7)
17. Everyday (5)
18. Boy with magic lamp (7)
19. Not seen (9)
20. Citrus fruit (5)
21. Single unit (3)
22. More recent (5)
23. Wipe out completely (9)
24. Extreme fear (6)
25. Groups of fruit trees (8)

LEVEL F

◆ ❓ ANSWER NO.2 ❓ ◆

PUZZLE 181

Look at the diagrams, crack the logic of the puzzle,
and discover the missing letters.

◆?◆ ANSWER NO.188 ◆?◆

PUZZLE 182

In the diagram you see the magic word Abracadabra spelt out as a pyramid. There are various paths from top to bottom but how many ways can you discover to spell the trick word?

A
BB
RRR
AAAA
CCCCC
AAAAAA
DDDDDDD
AAAAAAAA
BBBBBBBBB
RRRRRRRRRR
AAAAAAAAAAA

ANSWER NO.187

PUZZLE 183

Start at the top left square and fill in the answers to the clues. The LAST TWO letters of each word form the first two letters of the next word. Follow the grid in an ever-decreasing spiral to the centre.

A grid with numbered squares arranged in a spiral pattern:

1				2					
			8				9		3
			15				16		
7	14				20				
								10	
	13	19					17		
			18						4
				12		11			
		6					5		

1. Wild dog (6)
2. Water tortoise (8)
3. Discoverer of new ideas (8)
4. Musical instrument (5)
5. Story (8)
6. Used for long distance conversation (9)
7. Worn for decoration (8)
8. Eaten at breakfast (6)
9. Type of maths (7)
10. Demanded by kidnappers (6)
11. Sign to the superstitious (4)
12. Holds a letter (8)
13. Fruit (4)
14. Reach your destination (6)
15. Pest (6)
16. Crazy (6)
17. Closer (6)
18. Mistake (5)
19. Music makers (10)
20. To do with fortune telling using the stars (12)

LEVEL F

ANSWER NO.19

PUZZLE 184

Just a brief message, irritatingly obscure of course.
Can you work it out?

FYTHNKTHSSGNGTBS

YYHDBTTRTHNKAGN

 ANSWER NO.183

PUZZLE 185

Look at the word below. It's actually
Monrovian for 'Mine's a large cheeseburger
with extra relish.' No, that's a lie. But the letters do
have one strange property. What is it?

AAARGH!

EHIKOX

 ANSWER NO.186

PUZZLE 186

Look at the signpost below. The distances given are related, by some form of twisted logic, to the place names. Can you work out the logic and then replace the question mark with the correct distance?

ANSWER NO.178

PUZZLE 187

The letters in the computer screen make a series.
Work out the logic and replace the question mark.

PUZZLE 188

Five of the words below are related. Discover which ones they are and then see if heady could join them.

fireball

ready

it

yellow

transubstantiation

hamburger

analysis

anything

bottomless

acolyte

rival

rivet

golf

ANSWER NO.185

PUZZLE 189

Five of the words below are related. Discover which ones they are and then see if ability could join them.

ziggurat average

ear gizmo

introduction

onomatopoeia

xylophone

uncle

classic

hangman

numerical

depend force

grass white

PUZZLE 190

Look at the signpost below. The distances given are
related, by some form of twisted logic, to the place
names. Can you work out the logic and then replace
the question mark with the correct distance?

LEVEL F

Too many people knew the code to Joe's menu and he was losing a fortune in free pizza. Now he has a new code (still based on the value of letters). Can you crack it, discover the price of pancakes, and win a free hamburger?

Joe's Diner

Apple Pie :...$13.60

Icecream $15.90

Chocolate Cake....$24.90

Pancakes .... ?

PUZZLE 192

Look at the signpost below. The distances given are related, by some form of twisted logic, to the place names. Can you work out the logic and then replace the question mark with the correct distance? If you want a clue, remember that words have consonants and vowels.

CALIFORNIA 55

BAHAMAS   35

ESSEX ?

QUEBEC 33

PUZZLE 193

Walter is planning a holiday but is not quite sure where he's going. Can you help him by matching the country to the capital city.

PERU	CAIRO
BRUSSELS	NEW ZEALAND
TURKEY	BELGIUM
STOCKHOLM	ISTANBUL
EGYPT	WELLINGTON
SWEDEN	LIMA

AAARGH!

F

◇ ? ◇ ANSWER NO.74 ◇ ? ◇

ANSWERS

1

2
1. London.
2. Onion.
3. Once.
4. Cease.
5. Several.
6. Allow
7. Owner.
8. Erase.
9. Senior.
10. Order.
11. Era.
12. Astronomy.
13. Myrrh.
14. Rhyme.
15. Medicine.
16. Nervous.
17. Usual.
18. Aladdin.
19. Invisible.
20. Lemon.
21. One.
22. Newer.
23. Eradicate.
24. Terror.
25. Orchards.

3 Ascend, Battle, Arabia, Cheeky, Bronze, Eagles, Arctic, Boughs. The answer is Strength.

4 Creep, Alibi, Nails, Comic, Eagle, Rails. The signs of the zodiac are Cancer and Pisces.

5   Cinderella.

6   Indigo, Number,
Treaty, Race, India,
Glue, Umbrella,
Elephant.
The word is intrigue.

7   John Lennon
Helena
Bonham-Carter
Napoleon Bonaparte
Elizabeth Taylor
Neil Armstrong
Albert Einstein
Richard Gere.

8   Horse, Goats,
Mules,
Sheep, Ducks.

9   Red.

10   Swimming, Archery,
Football, Athletics,
Riding, Ice skating.
The word is Safari.

11   Knuckles, Ducklings,
Inklings, Pickling,
Includes.

12   George Bush
Charles Dickens
Demi Moore
Whitney Houston
Isaac Newton.

13   Too many cooks
spoil the broth.
A stich in time saves
nine.
It never rains but it
pours.
Rome wasn't built
in a day.
Birds of a feather
flock together.

14   Little Red Riding
Hood.

15   Sonic the
Hedgehog.

16   Smell, Maid,
Cheap,
Thank, Peace, Flog,
Weld, Beard.
The girl's name is
Michelle.

17 Arm, Head, Leg, Foot.

18 Lucy. (Captain Hook, Peter Pan, Christopher Robin, Humpty Dumpty, Mother Goose, Betty Botter).

19 See below.

20
1. Mar, Ram, Arm.
2. Art, Tar, Rat.
3. Spar, Pars, Raps, Rasp.
4. Miles, Slime, Smile, Limes.

21 Pizza, Chicken, Doughnut, Sandwich, Salad, Ice cream.

22 Dog, Goldfish, Rabbit.

19

23 Faint heart never
    won fair lady.
    A bird in the hand
    is worth two in the
    bush.
    Its no use crying
    over spilt milk.
    People who live in
    glass houses
    shouldn't
    throw stones.

24 Fast, Area, Sets,
    Task.

25 Become. The words
    start and end with
    consecutive letters
    of the alphabet, eg,
    AdverB, CarD,
    EngulF, etc.

26 Kirsty. It doesn't
    have the letter A
    in it.

27 Apes.

28
```
          P
      B   A   T
    C U   R E D
  F A N T A S Y
```

29 There's many a slip
    between cup and
    lip.
    Don't count your
    chickens before they
    hatch.
    Never judge a book
    by it's cover.
    Empty vessels make
    most noise.
    Be sure your sin will
    find you out.

30 Winona Ryder.

31 Tyrannosaurus Rex.

32 Eggs, as all the
    others are dairy
    products.
    August, as all the
    others have an 'R'
    in the month.
    Spider, as all the
    others are insects.

    Poland, as all the
    others are in the
    European Union.
    Nova Scotia, as all
    the others are in
    America.

Harley-Davidson,
as all the others
are cars.
Cambridge, as all
the others are rivers.
Cyclone, as all the
others are types of
cloud.

33 Apple, Norman,
Opera, Night,
Yellow, Mark,
Opium, Ugly, Sea.
The word is
anonymous.

34 Neigh, Snowy,
Ready
Thorn, Large.

35 Bulldog, Dogfish.

36 Father Christmas.

37 See next page.

38 Digit, Aeons, Cacti,
Knock, Acorn,
Aches, Alias, Bliss,
Crete.
The answer is
deckchair.

39 1. Mouse and
Gerbil.
2. Cat and Sheep.
3. Shark and Wasp.
4. Rabbit and
Horse.
5. Monkey and
Antelope.
6. Cow and Ape.
7. Dog and
Hamster.
8. Rat and Flea.

40 Rota, Nostril, Lair,
Joust.
The 10 letter word
is journalist.

41 Rumplestiltskin.

42 25.

43 Oliver Cromwell
Mahatma Gandhi
George Washington
William Cody
Michelle Pfeiffer
Julia Roberts
Robin Hood.

44 Catherine Wheel.

A	X	M	I	R	R	O	R	H
B	E	L	D	D	A	S	B	A
W	I	L	R	T	V	E	S	N
P	O	C	E	T	L	S	E	D
E	E	U	Y	L	J	B	K	L
M	E	D	S	C	A	L	O	E
A	G	W	A	N	L	M	P	B
R	E	V	Q	L	R	E	S	A
F	N	I	A	H	C	T	Y	R
D	R	A	U	G	D	U	M	S

ANSWERS

45 Unbearable.

46 Joust, Joist, Joint,
Point, Paint, Pains.
Clock, Cloak,
Croak, Creak,
Break, Bread.

47 Catfish, Plaice,
Marlin, Dolphin,
Haddock, Tunny,
Squid, Oyster.
All vowels are
replaced by X.

48 Angora
Basket
Candid
Cuddle
Damsel
Earwig,
Famous
Genius
Happen,
Jockey
Margin
Mislay,
Normal
Outlaw
Porter
Plural
Quaver
Sentry
Suffix
Voyage.

49 Green Card
Gorillas in the Mist
Some Like it Hot
Who's That Girl?
Hannah and her
Sisters
Mannequin
It's a Wonderful
Life
Star Wars
Always
Little Women.

50 Chinese, Arabic,
Italian, English,
Spanish.

51 And, Bat, Dad, Eat,
Bad, End.

52 Bare/Bear,
Hare/Hair,
Hart/Heart,
Deer/Dear,
Reed/Read,
Beet/Beat.

53 Ran.

54 Pa, Pan, Pane,
Panel.

55 See opposite.

56 Blunder, Brigand,
Audible, Rebound,
Garbled.

57 Copenhagen.

58 The Once and
Future King.
The House at Pooh
Corner.
How does your
garden grow.

I'll huff and I'll puff.

59 Adhesive, Advise, Advises, Ashes, Aside, Asides, Aide, Aides, Aids, Avid, Dash, Dashes, Dais, Daises, Devise, Devises, Dies, Dish, Dishes, Disease, Diva, Divas, Dive, Dives, Have, Haves, Head, Heads, Heavies, Heave, Heaved, Heaves, Heed, Heeds, Hide, Hides, Hiss, Hissed, Hive, Hies, Hived, Hives, Ease, Eased, Eases, Eaves, Evade, Evades, Eves, Said, Save, Saved, Saves, Sash, Shad, Shade, Shades, Shads, Shave, Shaved, Shaves, Sheave, Sheaved, Sheaves, Shed, Sheds, Shield, Shies, Seas, Seaside, Seeds, Seeds, Sees, Side, Sides, Sieve, Sieved, Sieves, Idea, Ideas, Ides, Vase, Vases, Vied, Vies, Visa, Visas.

55

BRIDGE
CROWN
TEMPLE
IRIS
LOBE
NAPE
PALM
ARCH

60 Portugal, Hungary, Romania, Germany, Greece.

61 E.

62 Vermicelli.
This is a food.

63 To be or not to be,
That is the question.
(The first and last letters are removed).

64 Scatter.

65 S. (The first letter of Monday, Tuesday, etc.)

66 Idaho.

67 Journey to the Centre of the Earth.
The Last of the Mohicans.
Twenty Thousand Leagues Under the Sea.
The Little House on the Prairie.

On Her Majesty's Secret Service.

68
1. Phantom of the Opera.
2. Carousel.
3. Evita.
4. Starlight Express.
5. The Sound of Music.
6. Les Miserables.
7. Chess.
8. Miss Saigon.
9. Rocky Horror Show.
10. Cats.

69 Acrobatic.

70 Barter, Balloon, Create, Trader, Looter, Berate.

71 United States of America.

72 Across
1. Mast
6. Orphan
8. Pa
9. Rear

10. Ruler
12. Drinks
13. Do
14. Hill
16. Stag
18. Gel
19. Foal
21. Door
23. Corridor.

Down
1. Morning
2. Are
3. Spark
4. Thrush
5. Bandit
7. Needle
11. Roller
15. Igloo
16. Sap
17. Also
19. Far
20. Add
22. Or.

73 1. Inverted
2. Falsehood
3. Chivalrous
4. Famished
5. Vanish
6. Meteor
7. Chortle

8. Spouse
9. Caprice
10. Permitted

74 Peru, Lima
New Zealand,
Wellington
Belgium, Brussels,
Turkey, Istanbul
Sweden, Stockholm
Egypt, Cairo.

75 Cormorant
Crow
Cuckoo
Chaffinch
Canary.

76 See next page.

77 Back.

78 Andre Agassi.

79 Aches.

80 The correct order is
omen, pole, fork,
knee.
The word is moon.

P¹	G²	Y³	R⁴	H⁵	T⁶	A⁷	W⁸	I⁹	N¹⁰	E¹¹	V¹²	K¹³
Q¹⁴	U¹⁵	O¹⁶	B¹⁷	Z¹⁸	J¹⁹	D²⁰	M²¹	C²²	X²³	L²⁴	S²⁵	F²⁶

81 The correct order is shop, away need, down.
Sand is found on the beach.

82 Read down the eighth column from the left, the first letter is on the third line.

83 Settler, Letters.

84 Show and Sow
Open and Pen
Front and Font
Insane and Inane
Fear and Far
Cap and Carp
Neat and Net
Damp and Amp
Rain and Ran
Pest and Pet
Chop and Cop.
Sauce: Horseradish.

85 Money, Honey, Phoney, Phone, Home, Hole, Mole.

86 1. Alice in Wonderland.
2. Tom Sawyer.
3. Dracula.
4. Gulliver's Travels.
5. The Witches.

87 Bob, Bobs, Bobsleigh, Bosh, Bole, Boles, Boil, Boils, Bog, Bogs, Bogie, Bogies, Blob, Blobs, Beg, Begs, Bib, Bibs, Bible, Bibles, Bile, Bilge, Big, Oblige, Obliges, Obeli, Oil, Oils Ogle, Ogles, Ohs, Sob, Sol, Sole,

ANSWERS

Soli, Soil, Soh, Slob,
Sloe, Slog, Sleigh,
Silo, Sigh, Shoe,
She, Lob, Lobbies,
Lobs, Lobe, Lobes,
Lose, Log, Logs,
Loge, Loges, Lei,
Leis, Leg, Legs, Lib,
Lie, Lies, Ebb,
Ebbs, Ego, Egos,
Isle, Gob, Gobs,
Gobble, Gobbles,
Goch, Goes, Glob,
Giobs, Globe,
Globes, Glib, Gel,
Gels, Gib, Gibboxe,
Gibs, Gibe, Gibes,
Hob, Hobble,
Hobbles, Hobbies,
Hobs, Hose, Hole,
Holes, Holies, Hoe,
Hoes, Hog, Hogs,
His, Hie, Hies.

88 Teacher, Cheater,
Hectare.

89 Abdomen,
Bureaucrat,
Diversion,
Flabbergast,
Indicate,
Longitude,
Newspaper,
Romantic,
Sustenance,
Volunteer.

90 T. (The first letter
of one, two three
etc.)

91 No. The words in
the box each begins
with one of the
vowels in
their usual order.

92 Italy, Napoleon,
Douglas, Indigo,
Apple, Nightmare,
Algebra, Jerusalem,
Ostrich, Neptune,
Emperor, Salami.
The character is
Indiana Jones.

93 California, Idaho
Nebraska, Hawaii,
Alaska.

94 Raiders of the Lost
Ark.

ANSWERS

T	A	B	E	A	R	G	S	G	A
P	C	O	D	F	O	T	S	H	B
A	G	O	T	R	Q	U	N	V	D
R	T	H	F	L	M	N	A	W	R
R	C	I	D	E	S	A	K	K	A
O	R	S	G	T	U	N	E	L	P
T	A	V	T	E	C	B	O	P	O
U	G	Z	Q	S	R	L	J	R	E
H	I	Y	E	K	N	O	M	E	L
C	E	L	E	P	H	A	N	T	D

95 Rain, Snow, Hail, Mist.

96 Spare
Pears
Reaps
Pares
Spear.

97 Rocking Horse.

98 Four, Seven, One, Six. When added together they make eighteen.

99 Sarah, Fiona, George, James.

100 Play time.

101 Earwig, Centipede, Tarantula,

Cockroach,
Earthworm.

102 See previous page.

103 Denmark,
Canada,
Germany, Ireland,
New Zealand.

104 Robinson Crusoe
Swiss Family
    Robinson
The Three
    Musketeers
Tales of Tom
    Bombadil
The Chronicles of
    Narnia.

105 Iceland.

106 She said that that
'that' that I said
should have been
'those.'

The culprit made
his admission
sorrowfully.
The day after he
was shot.

I said 'and' but he
said I said 'but,' but
he was wrong and I
said so.

107 Scorned. (All the
words contain
food.)

108 Noiseless Lionesses.

109 1. Computer.
2. Sinai.
3. Cathedral.
4. Pizza.
5. Goldfish.
6. Ostrich.
7. Magazine.
8. Bicycle.

110 Ursa Major
Orion
Horse Nebula
Neptune
Venus
Betelgeuse
Pluto
Perseids
Halley's Comet.

111
1. All that glitters (glisters) is not gold.
2. A rolling stone gathers no moss.
3. The grass is always greener on the other side of the fence.
4. Set a thief to catch a thief.
5. Troubles always seems to come in threes.

112 Butter
Totter
Barrel
Longer
Rubble
Totals.

113 Hand.

114 Accountant, Pilot, Teacher, Nurse, Discjockey.

115 Bedtime story.

116 Herd, Clutch, Gaggle, Pride, School.

117
1. Attention
2. Nitrogen
3. Nugget
4. Tolerable
5. Eerie
6. Eggplant
7. Tortoise
8. Eyewitness
9. Squabble
10. Execution
11. Nothing.

118 Chestnut
Lime
Redwood
Laburnum
Douglas Fir

119 Catapult. (All the words include the name of an animal.)

120 Here we go round the Mulberry Bush.
What big eyes you have Grand mama.
The Lion, the Witch and the Wardrobe.

Little Bo Peep she
lost her sheep.

121 A B E H I.

122 Snake, Ache, Bake,
Rake, Wake,
Forsake, Lake,
Break, Stake,
Fake.

123 The Hobbit –
J.R.R. Tolkien
James and the
Giant Peach
– Roald Dahl,
The House at Pooh
Corner – A.A. Milne
Finn Family
Moomintroll
– Tove Jannson
Tom Sawyer
– Mark Twain
White Fang
– Jack London.

124 1. Rain
2. Sun
3. Snow
4. Hail.

125 Pimento. This is
also the name of a
food.

126 The correct order is
wolf, taxi, hair,
ache.Fire is the
thing which is hot.

127 To swim like a fish
To fly like a bird
To rain cats and
dogs
To run like the wind
To smell like a rose.

128 Primrose
Buttercup
Daisy
Bluebell
Heather.

129 Rotate
Succulent
Dishwasher
Hostile
Nocturnal
Frontier
Lacerate
Unfurl
Misjudge
Quarterly

130 Saxophone.

131 Modicum
Cadmium
Academic
Dummied
Acceded.

132 Bugs, (all curved letters – no straight lines).

133 1. Harvard
2. Bangkok
3. Buttercup
4. Marsupial
5. Roulette
6. Diamond
7. Deciduous
8. Scotland
9. Cannibal
10. Planet.

134 Farmer
Fields
Horses
Cereal
Fences.

135 Sea of Tranquility.

136 Oblique
Infinity
Arrogance
Convalesce
Millennium
Subliminal
Humanoid
Ingenuity
Rudimentary
Bouquet.

137 Bill and Ted's Excellent Adventure.
Around the World in Eighty Days.
The Purple Rose of Cairo.
My Stepmother is an Alien.
The Importance of Being Earnest.

138 See next page.

139 Loyal,
Spoil
Royal
Toil
Gargoyle.

140 Fridge
Microwave
Kettle
Oven
Saucer.

141 Disaster.

142 Blackguard
Blueberry

Blueprint
Blackbeard
Greenhouse

143 Ate pill.

144 Green Brian
(Big Ben, Old Glory,
Union Jack,
Blue Beard
Stormin' Norman).

138

145 See below.
Theme is the word
that appears twice.

146 First
Fist
Sift
Lift
Flit
Fit
Fig.

147 Tom Cruise.

145

148 Cat, Ant, Rat, Bat, Dog.

149
1. Just in time.
2. Cloud burst.
3. Isabel.
4. Shipwreck.
5. One thing after another.
6. Step by step.
7. Fiddler on the Roof.
8. The last resort.
9. Piggy in the middle.
10. Mixed nuts.
11. Young at Heart.
12. Jumble sale.
13. Rule the roost

150 E. (The second letter of January, February, March etc.)

151 The correct order is bird, book, vase, chef. The flower is rose.

152 Staple, Pastel, Palest, Plates, Pleats, Petals.

153 Latin.

154 Bugle, Attack, Tank Tactics, Lieutenant, Enemy.
The word is battle.

155 Mother Goose.

156 Elation, All, Slope, Pasta, Red, Ordain, Barrier.
Breeds of Dog: Spaniel, Poodle, Alsatian, Labrador, Terrier.

157
1. Hockey.
2. Cycling.
3. Badminton.
4. Riding.
5. Karate.
6. Skating.

158 Ski, Camp, Hail, Ocean, Olden, Lapel. The answer is school.

ANSWERS

```
M     N O S B I G E I B B E D
  I         T                 C A
    C       A N N O D A M R N   K   L
    H H   K   A           I Y   I   A
    S A E   E       R     R G E   T E
N P E     R T   E   G P   H R     R N E
O I L S       H     D Y   T A     A O L
T L J     I   A         A M S C P M   R S
S L A     N T         J   A H M     E I
U I C     E N V O G U E   I A E     D L
O H K C O L B E H T N O S D I K W E N R
H P S       E D           F R A     A A
Y N O       R   Y         R A R     X C
E O N     I   E   H       E M A     E A
N S     V     M   T   D   T     L D
T L     O   X R A M D R A H C I R   A N
I I     J               C         I I
H W N E E T S G N I R P S E C U R B   L
W O   B O B B Y B R O W N           E
B                 L E O J Y L L I B
```

159
1. Mansfield Park
   – Jane Austen.
2. Hard Times
   – Charles
   Dickens.
3. Romeo and Juliet
   – William
   Shakespeare.
4. Tess of the
   d'Urbervilles
   – Thomas
   Hardy.

160 Denmark, Iran,
Canada, Germany,
China.

161 Light
Spark
Shine
Gleam
Flame.

162 Igloo.

163 See previous page. Janet Jackson is missing.

164 Electric, Longer, Ember, Cricket, Tablet, Rosemary, Oregano, Dawdle, Eternal.
The word is electrode.

165 A.

166 Teddy bear.

167 Cat, Dog, Fish, Hamster.

168 Laura, Freddy, Sally, Tony.

169 Too many chiefs and not enough Indians.
Many hands make light work.
An apple a day keeps the doctor away.
A new broom sweeps clean.
A stitch in time saves nine.
Cut your coat according to your cloth.
When the cat's away the mouse will play.
Can't see the wood for the trees.
All's well that ends well.
It's an ill wind that blows nobody any good.

170 32.

171 Large elephants seldom walk quickly.
Hamsters never take lunch with crocodiles.
Even small giraffes sleep standing.
Beautiful butterflies flitter among flowers.
Giant pandas dwell among bamboo groves.

All the words have their first halves after their second.

172 1. It's an ill wind that blows nobody any good.
2. All work and no play makes Jack a dull boy.
3. Too many cooks spoil the broth.
4. You can't make a silk purse out of a sow's ear.
5. It never rains but it pours.

173 Bel (Bombay Duck, Catfish, Haddock, Piranha, Barracuda).

174 Vincent Van Gogh
Leonardo da Vinci
Pablo Picasso
John Constable
Marc Chagall.

175 Palace, Cottage, Bungalow, Castle, Monastery.
Cedar, Redwood, Hickory, Maple, Hornbeam.

176 The Wizard of Oz.
Close Encounters of the Third Kind.
Pollyanna.
Back to the Future.
National Velvet.
Batman Returns.
Beauty and the Beast.
Honey I Shrunk the Kids.
The Sound of Music.
Jurassic Park.

177 1. Twenty and Seven.
2. Million and One.
3. Three and Eight.
4. Two and Nine.
5. Four and Ten.

178 Consonants are worth 3, vowels 12.

Therefore Yale should be 30 miles away.

179 The five words (Average, Ear, Introduction, Onomatopoeia, Uncle) all begin with vowels. Ability fits.

180 Consonants are worth 7, vowels 8. Therefore Beijing is 53 miles away.

181 Consonants are worth 2, vowels 9. Therefore Essex is 24 miles away.

182 The letters are valued in reverse alphabetical order (A=26, B=25, etc) and multiplied by 10. Pancakes cost $14.60.

183 If you think this is going to be easy you had better think again. (All the vowels have been removed.)

184 The numbers above the line are all three-letter words.

185 All the words (Ready, Anything, Yellow, Analysis, Acolyte) contain Y. Heady fits.

186 When vertically reversed they remain the same.

187 Only one, of course. We did tell you it was a trick!

188 F, M, N. (Initial letters of months.)

189 $7.80. A=1, B=2, C=3, etc. Then multiply the result by 10.

190 The five words (Anteater, Eagles, Ahead, Azalea, Nausea) all have EA in them. Confidence won't fit.

191 Consonants are worth 4, vowels 2, therefore Washington DC is 42 miles away.

192 They are all composed of letters which, when laterally reversed, remain the same.

193 The five words (Beach, Beans, Cease, Again, Drama) all have an A in the middle. Brass therefore fits.